music minus one 'cello

GREAT SCOTT!
ragtime minus YOU

Scott Joplin
NEW RAG
MAPLE LEAF RAG
THE NONPAREIL
THE EASY WINNERS
STOPTIME RAG

Scott Joplin - Louis Chauvin
HELIOTROPE BOUQUET

Tom Turpin
HARLEM RAG, TWO STEP

Joseph Glover
HURRICANE RAG

Luckey Roberts
MUSIC BOX RAG

Eubie Blake
CHEVY CHASE

3708

Metronome taps have been added to this recording. These taps indicate the tempo of the music immediately following.

If you listen carefully while following your music, you will see how the taps cue your entrances. This system has been followed throughout the recording.

Be aware that music in slow 2/4 is often played with a feeling of four beats to the measure.

Printed in Canada

(Minus You)

Chevy Chase

CELLO
4 Beats (1 measure)
precede music

Music by Eubie Blake
Arranged by William Zinn

MMO CD 3708

GREYSCALE

BIN TRAVELER FORM

Cut By _Jose O._ Qty_____ Date_____

Scanned By _Khatie_ Qty_____ Date _9/23_

Scanned Batch IDs

_796289391_   _796286996_   _____

Notes / Exception

_____

_____

_____

_____

_____

Chevy Chase

Pg. 5

New Rag

CELLO
4 Beats (2 measures)
precede music ♩ = 106

Allegro Moderato

Music by Scott Joplin
Arranged by William Zinn

New Rag

Music Box Rag

CELLO
4 Beats (1 measure)
precede music ♩ = 130

Music by Luckey Roberts
Arranged by William Zinn

Music Box Rag

Pg. 9

Harlem Rag
Two Step

CELLO
No Beats precede
music.

Music by Tom Turpin
Arranged by William Zinn

CELLO

Harlem Rag

Pg. 11

Maple Leaf Rag

Maple Leaf Rag

Trio

Heliotrope Bouquet

CELLO
No beats
precede music
♩ = 109
Slow March Tempo

Music by Scott Joplin
& Louis Chauvin
Arranged by William Zinn

Heliotrope Bouquet

Pg. 15

The Nonpareil

The Nonpareil

Stoptime Rag

Stoptime Rag

Pg. 19

The Easy Winners

CELLO
No beats
precede music

Music by Scott Joplin
Arranged by William Zinn

MMO CD 3708

CELLO

The Easy Winners

Hurricane Rag

Music by Joseph Glover
Arranged by William Zinn

MMO CD 3708

Hurricane Rag

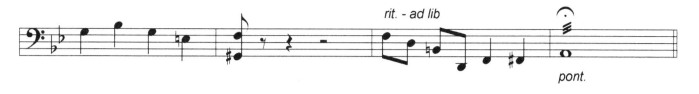

GREAT SCOTT!
ragtime minus YOU

Scott Joplin
NEW RAG
MAPLE LEAF RAG
THE NONPAREIL
THE EASY WINNERS
STOPTIME RAG

Scott Joplin - Louis Chauvin
HELIOTROPE BOUQUET

Tom Turpin
HARLEM RAG, TWO STEP

Joseph Glover
HURRICANE RAG

Luckey Roberts
MUSIC BOX RAG

Eubie Blake
CHEVY CHASE

3708

MMO Music Group • 50 Executive Boulevard, Elmsford, New York 10523, 1-(800) 669-7464
Website: www. minusone.com • E-mail: mmomus@aol.com